grasshopper

grasshop

ROTHERHAM LIBRARY AND INFORMATION SERVICES

This book must be returned by the date specified at the time of issue as the DATE DUE for RETURN.

The loan may be extended (personally, by post or telephone) for a further period, if the book is not required by another reader, by quoting the above number/author/title.

LIS 7a

round-beetle (*Caloso idum*), natural size.

a, male, dorsal view ; *b*, female, lateral view.

A Species of *Phrynus*, about life-size.

Eurygaster alternatus; wings partly open. (Line shows natural size.)

Thighed Metapodius (*Metapodius femoratus*).

Bombardier-beetle (*Brachinus stygicornis*). (Vertical line shows natural size.)

hemeridæ. opean May=fly (*Eph- gata*) and its sub- va.

Spiderwort Owlet-moth (*Prodenia flavimedia*). *a*, larva ; *b*, wings of moth.

The Cucujo.

Apple-sn *pullar* *s*, siphon; *esses* *culn*

The Cl stem l *a*, larv ting in ver = ste the bee

np

Homo Tail of a ing homoc dal verteb dal rays; bones; *p*, esses of ca united to f for the aor ral spines.

Podisus placidus. *a*, enlarged ; *b*, natural size.

Libellulidæ. Development of a dragon=fly, showing the subaquatic larva, emergence from the pupa, and he adult fully winged insect.

hymata erosa.

A Flea (*Pulex irritans*). *a*, puncturing stylets of the proboscis.

A Bristletail (*Lepisma saccharina*). $5/1$

Bacon= beet'e.

One of th oni

Atypus sulzeri. (Vertical line shows natural size.)

Grape-vine Fidia (*F. viticida*). (Line sh ws natural size.)

a

A Derm

per

by

Ting Morris

• • • • • • • •

illustrated by

Desiderio Sanzi

designed by

Deb Miner

W

FRANKLIN WATTS
LONDON • SYDNEY

When you are out in a field or meadow on a sunny summer day, you can often hear loud chirping sounds. It's as if you are surrounded by invisible musicians. But if you move toward the sounds, the chirping usually stops.

Who are these strange musicians? And how do they make their music? **Turn the page and take a closer look.**

There he is – a little green grasshopper was making all that noise.

He's hard to spot in the long grass, and now he's keeping very still and quiet because he felt your footsteps from a long way off. If he sees you, he'll leap in the air and land a few metres away.

That's an amazing jump for such a small creature. If you could leap like a grasshopper, you'd cover almost 30 metres in one jump!

AN OUTSIDE SKELETON

Like other insects, grasshoppers have no backbone. Their skeleton (called an exoskeleton) is on the outside of their body.

WHAT ARE GRASSHOPPERS?

Grasshoppers and their relatives – locusts, katydids, and crickets – are insects. They live in grassy places all over the world, but they like it best in warm climates. The difference between grasshoppers and crickets is the size of their antennae. A grasshopper's antennae are short, and a cricket's are long.

A GRASSHOPPER'S BODY

A grasshopper's body has three parts – the HEAD, the THORAX and the ABDOMEN.

Grasshoppers have five EYES: two large compound eyes and three small eyes – one below each feeler and one in between. Each compound eye is made up of thousands of tiny lenses, so grasshoppers can see all around.

The two feelers (called ANTENNAE) are the grasshopper's nose. The MOUTH has two strong jaws.

A grasshopper has six LEGS and uses all of them when it walks. Powerful muscles in the back legs push it forward when it jumps. Most grasshoppers have two pairs of WINGS. Legs and wings are attached to the thorax.

The abdomen is made up of segments, which allows it to bend and twist easily.

Grasshoppers breathe through 10 pairs of breathing holes, called SPIRACLES. These holes are along the sides of the abdomen and the thorax.

Female grasshoppers have an OVIPOSITOR, or egg placer, at the end of their abdomen.

ANTENNAE

SIMPLE EYES

HEAD

COMPOUND EYE

KNEE JOINT

WINGS

MOUTH

THORAX

SPIRACLES

ABDOMEN

OVIPOSITOR

7

This grasshopper is snacking on fresh grass.

He chews through a blade, then climbs onto the next stem, then the next and the next. With their strong jaws, grasshoppers eat through leaves and flowers very quickly and can cause a lot of damage. But this green grasshopper is harmless.

He usually feeds on the grass along country paths and roads. Don't try to pick him up. If he feels threatened, he might bite you.

WHAT'S ON THE MENU?

There are plenty of leaves to eat in fields and meadows. Some grasshoppers eat only certain kinds of plants, but others are not as fussy. On a sunny day, one grasshopper can go through a lot of grass, and 50 grasshoppers can eat as much as a cow! That's why they can become a pest to farmers and gardeners.

MATCHING COLOURS

Grasshoppers match the colour of their surroundings. Those that live among green leaves are green, and those that live near the ground are usually brownish.

A SIDEWAYS CHEW

Grasshoppers hold plants with their front legs while their saw-like jaws chew them up. The jaws are on the outside of the mouth and move from side to side. Its upper lip is in front of the jaws, and its lower lip – with the grasshopper's taste buds – is behind the jaws.

9

Grasshoppers are famous for their musical sounds, but they don't form a band. They live on their own and sing to attract a female mate. Some grasshoppers chirp along with others just for the fun of it. **This grasshopper is starting up his little song.** It sounds a bit like an alarm clock ringing, but he hasn't woken anyone and there's no answer to his call.

LOCUSTS

Locusts are big grasshoppers that grow up to 5 centimetres long. They live in warm climates. Locusts have a bad reputation because swarms of millions of them can eat their way through whole fields of crops. But when there are only a few of them, they are harmless.

YOUTH GROUPS

Young locusts, or hoppers, crowd together and live as a group. Then they meet other groups and march in great numbers over the land, eating every plant on the way. Their colour changes from brown to black and yellow, and their wings grow strong. When they are fully grown, they form huge swarms and fly to where there is plenty to eat.

FROM THE DESERT

Swarms of desert locusts build up in Africa. The young have longer wings and brighter colours than locusts that don't swarm. They fly hundreds of miles with the wind. When a swarm lands, it can eat up to 100,000 tonnes of food in a day.

11

MUSICAL LEGS

Grasshoppers do not have voices, as we do. They make sounds by rubbing their back legs against their front wings. On the inside of each back leg is a row of tiny pegs. The grasshopper rubs the hard edge of its front wing across the pegs. Try rubbing the edge of a card against the teeth of a comb to see how it works!

The grasshopper has moved to a different spot, hoping for a better reception. He bursts into a new song, ticking, rattling and chirping. The noise gets louder and louder, and then suddenly he stops. At first there's silence, followed by a few quiet chirps. The grasshopper hears them and replies with a new song. Can you see who he's calling?

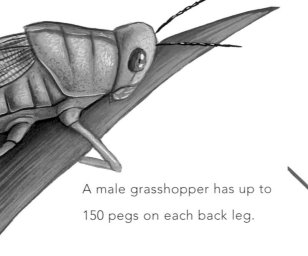

12

A male grasshopper has up to 150 pegs on each back leg.

MUSICAL CRICKETS

Crickets are slightly different from grasshoppers. Males sing by rubbing the toothed edges of their front wings together. Females hear the call with ears in their front legs. A small swelling just below the knee is the cricket's ear.

HOW DO GRASSHOPPERS HEAR?

Grasshoppers' ears are on the sides of their abdomen, beneath the wings. They are small patches that pick up the slightest sounds.

KATY-DID, KATY-DID!

Katydids are a kind of North American bush cricket. They get their name from their song, which sounds as if they were calling "Katy did, katy did!" They sing on warm evenings and sometimes go on all night.

While the female grasshopper was listening to the male's call, a wasp swooped down and stung her. Now she can't move her legs or use her wings – the wasp's poisonous sting has had its effect. **There's nothing the male grasshopper can do, and he jumps as high as he can to get away from a possible wasp attack.** Look at him flying through the air!

FIGHTING BACK

Grasshoppers escape from their enemies by jumping or flying away. They can also bite, and some spit an unpleasant brown liquid, called tobacco juice, at their attackers.

GRASSHOPPER HUNTERS

Sand wasps capture grasshoppers. They paralyse them with a sting and carry the body to their hole in the sand. They feed the grasshoppers to their young.

WARNING COLOURS

Some grasshoppers have brightly coloured bodies or flash their wings to warn enemies to keep their distance.

INVISIBLE

This katydid has the colour and shape of the leaf on which it perches. The veins in its wings make them look like leaves.

15

The field cricket is not as peaceful as the grasshopper. The male lives alone in a hole and fiercely guards his territory against any rival who dares to come near him. When this happens, they try to bite each other, and the battle usually ends with the death of one or both of them. The male's fighting song is quite different from his mating song.

The green grasshopper is not the only one chirping in this field. **There are lots of other songsters about.** But the females don't get confused, because every kind of grasshopper has a slightly different song. This female knows the songs of her own kind and chooses the one who sings the best – and the loudest!

THOUSANDS OF GRASSHOPPERS

There are about 9,000 different kinds of grasshoppers in the world. The largest is more than 25 centimetres in length, and the smallest is just 6 millimetres long.

NO FIGHTING!

Male grasshoppers never fight each other. Rival chirping – a sort of grasshoppers' song contest – keeps them apart.

A PRESENT FOR KATY

The male katydid usually gives a present of food to the female when they meet to mate. Katydids feed on insects, so the gift is a tasty bug.

After mating, the female grasshopper looks for good places to lay her eggs. From the end of summer until autumn, she's busy digging holes, then filling and sealing them.

A special pointed tube at the tip of her abdomen does all the work. She uses it to dig deep holes under the grass, then lays about 10 eggs in each one and covers them with a sticky froth. Once this is hard, it's waterproof and it keeps the eggs safe through the winter. Young grasshoppers will crawl out of these holes next summer, but the parents won't live through the winter to see their young.

EGG CAPSULE

Locusts lay their eggs in a long, thin capsule of more than 100 eggs.

LOOK-ALIKES

Depending on the weather, grasshopper eggs hatch in May or June – the warmer the weather, the earlier they hatch. Newborn grasshoppers, called nymphs, look like miniature adults but without the wings. They start feeding on grass immediately after hatching.

The eggs have hatched in the spring sunshine, and now tiny grasshoppers are growing up everywhere. Some of the young are only as big as a grain of rice, but they look just like their grasshopper parents. As they grow, they change their skin. A new, more comfortable skin grows beneath the old one. The wings are still missing, but they'll be in place by the final skin change.

Look at this little fellow. He's outgrown his baby suit for the fifth time and is now an adult. He's pumping up his new wings. **In minutes, he'll be ready for takeoff.**

LOOKING PALE

Newly-moulted grasshoppers are a white or yellowish colour when they crawl out of their old skin. They take a while to develop more colour. Green bush-crickets and katydids come out green at every change. They eat the old skin that has split.

GROWING AND CHANGING

It takes between one and two months for a young grasshopper to reach adult size. During this time, it changes its skin five or six times. This is called moulting. Each time the skin gets too tight, it splits. A new skin has grown beneath the old one. Crickets sometimes moult more than 10 times.

22

GROWN UP AT LAST

The grasshopper's last change takes about an hour:

The grasshopper finds a strong plant and clings firmly to the stem upside-down.

The skin behind its head starts to split, and the grasshopper slides out of its old see-through covering. First it pushes out its head, then it pulls out its front legs. It's hard work!

Pulling out the long back legs is not at all easy. Once they are out, the grasshopper takes a rest. It is held up by the end of its body, which is still inside its old skin.

Now it reaches up, grips the old skin tightly, and pulls the end of its body out. Free at last!

The grasshopper is now the right way up. It holds on to the old skin. It cannot jump away yet, because its body is still wet and its wings are soft and crumpled. It pumps blood into its wings, and after a few minutes they are much bigger. When its body is dry and the wings are hard and strong, it will leap into the air and onto fresh grass to feed.

There will be no more baby hops for this grasshopper. **He's ready for some big leaps, and every jump is powered by his wings.** You can tell this by the gentle fluttering sound his wings make as he jumps. Ahead of him is a summer of sunshine, tasty grass, and chirpy songs. This year's musicians sound just like their parents, even though they had no lessons.

A GIANT LEAP

Large muscles in the back legs push the grasshopper forward and shoot it up into the air. In mid-leap, the grasshopper opens its wings and flies a short distance before dropping down again. By using its wings as well as its legs, a grasshopper can jump even further.

PROTECTIVE WINGS

A grasshopper's tough front wings protect the large back wings. When not in use, the back wings fold up like fans under the front wings.

FLYING WINGS

The thin back wings are mainly used for flying. When the grasshopper flies, it flaps its wings rapidly.

A male and female
grasshopper mate.

Grasshopper

A male
grasshopper
sings to
attract a mate.

After the nymph's final moult,
it is an adult grasshopper.

The female grasshopper
lays eggs.

The eggs
hatch into
nymphs.

CIRCLE OF LIFE

The nymphs shed their
skin, or moult, as they grow.

bush cricket A cricket with long antennae; it is sometimes called a long-horned grasshopper.

climates Weather conditions usually found in a particular place.

compound eye An eye made up of thousands of tiny lenses.

fertilize To cause a female insect's eggs to develop into young.

field cricket A European cricket that lives in a burrow in grasslands.

katydids Several different kinds of North American crickets.

lenses Transparent structures that focus light in eyes.

nymphs The young form of grasshoppers after they hatch from eggs.

paralyse To make an animal unable to move, often by stinging or biting it.

segments The many parts into which something is divided.

sperm Fluid produced by male animals that makes a female's eggs grow into young.

swarms Large numbers of insects that stay close and move together.

taste buds Cells on the surface of the lower lip that allow a grasshopper to taste things.

territory An area that is patrolled by a male insect and defended against other males.

INDEX

An Appleseed Editions book

First published in 2004 by Franklin Watts
96 Leonard Street, London, EC2A 4XD

Franklin Watts Australia
45–51 Huntley Street, Alexandria, NSW 2015

© 2004 Appleseed Editions

Created by Appleseed Editions Ltd,
Well House, Friars Hill, Guestling, East Sussex, TN35 4ET

Illustrator: Desiderio Sanzi

Designer: Deb Miner

ISBN 0 7496 5704 9

A CIP catalogue for this book
is available from the British Library.

Printed and bound in the USA

Head of Blind-
worm. 1/2

A Book-scorpion
(*Chelifer can-
croides*). 5/1

a
Cotton-stainer.

Epeiridæ.
a, male, and *b*, fe-
male, of *Epeira stel-
lata; c*, characteristic
orb-web of an epeirid
(*Epeira strix*).

b

The I
Drag
(*Dra
eatus*

Click-beetle,
natural size.

Proxys punctulatus.

Agonoderus dorsalis (Le Conte).
Vertical line shows natural size.

Hawthorn-tingis
arcuata), one of the
enlarged about ten t

Parasite of the Beaver (*Platy-
psyllus castoris*). (Line shows
natural size.)

a

Hellgrammite (*a*)
and Hellgrammite-
fly.

The Twig-gir-
dler (*Oncideres
cingulata*). 1/1
a, a branch girdled by the beetle.

Sinea diadema, one
of the *Reduviidæ.*
(Line shows natural
size.)

The Bait-bug.

Rose-beetle (*Cetonia aurata*).
Vertical line shows natural size.

Flour-beetle (*Te
litor*). (Line sho
size.)

Galeruca notata
(Line shows natural size.)

Pill-beetle (*Byrrh*

Ground-beetle (*Caloso...lidum*), natural size.

Eurygaster alternatus; wings partly open. (Line shows natural size.)

Thighed Metapodius (*Metapodius femoratus*).

Spiderwort Owlet-moth (*Prodenia flavimedia*). *a*, larva; *b*, wings of moth.

b

a

The Cucujo.

Bombardier-beetle (*Brachinus stygicornis*). (Vertical line shows natural size.)

a

b

Podisus placidus. *a*, enlarged; *b*, natural size.

phemeridæ. ropean May-fly (*Eph...ulgata*) and its sub...rva.

A Bristletail (*Lepisma saccharina*). 5/1

A Flea (*Pulex irritans*). *a*, puncturing stylets of the proboscis.

a

Libellulidæ. Development of a dragon-fly, showing the subaquatic larva, emergence from the pupa, and the adult fully winged insect.

Phymata erosa.

Atypus sulzeri. (Vertical line shows natural size.)

Bacon-beet'e.

Grape-vine Fidia (*F. viticida*). (Line shows natural size.)

The stem *a*, lar...ting i... ver-s... the be...

Hom... Tail of... ing homo... dal verte... dal rays... bones; *p*... esses of... united to... for the ac... ral spines...

One of t... on...

A De... Larva... beetle (*b*...